Bugs A to Z

by Terri DeGezelle

Consultant:
Mark O'Brien,
Collections Coordinator,
Museum of Zoology,
Division of Insects,
University of Michigan,
Ann Arbor

A+ Books

Capstone Curriculum Publishing
Mankato, Minnesota

Aa

Ants and aphids are like farmers and cows. Aphids drink sap from plants and make a sweet milk called honeydew. Ants milk aphids to get honeydew to drink.

Ants and Aphids

Bb

Bedbug

Can you imagine a whole day without any food to eat? Bedbugs can live for months without food. When they do eat, they take a bite from birds, dogs, and even people. Ouch!

Cc

The centipede's name means *one hundred legs*, but most centipedes are born with 14 legs. As they get older, most centipedes grow 16 more legs. Hey! That adds up to 30 legs—why are they called centipedes?

Centipede

Aa Bb **Cc** Dd Ee Ff Gg Hh Ii Jj Kk Ll Mm Nn Oo Pp Qq Rr Ss Tt Uu Vv Ww Xx Yy Zz

Dd

Dragonfly

Dragonflies have two sets of wings. Each wing can move in a different direction and at a different speed, at the same time!

Ee

Earwig

The mother earwig stays with her eggs until they hatch. Then she feeds them food that she eats and then throws up. Think of it as bug baby food.

The body of the firefly can light up only when it flies. The firefly uses flashes of light to find a mate. The light it makes is cold light. Its light does not get hot like a lightbulb.

Ff

Firefly

Gg

Grasshoppers are music makers. They make music by rubbing their legs against their wings. Other grasshoppers can hear the music up to a mile away.

Grasshopper

Aa Bb Cc Dd Ee Ff **Gg** Hh Ii Jj Kk Ll Mm Nn Oo Pp Qq Rr Ss Tt Uu Vv Ww Xx Yy Zz

Hh

Honeybee

Honeybees gather nectar from flowers to make honey. After a bee finds a place to gather nectar, it flies back to the hive and dances. The dance tells other bees where to find the nectar.

Ii

The inchworm inches its back feet forward until they bump into its front feet. Then, the inchworm moves its front feet ahead until it cannot move them any farther. Then, it starts all over again.

Inchworm

Jj

Jewel Beetle

A young jewel beetle must shed its hard skin to grow. It does this by making its body bigger. This breaks the old skin and it falls away. Each time, a new, harder skin grows to replace it until the jewel beetle is fully grown.

Aa Bb Cc Dd Ee Ff Gg Hh Ii **Jj** Kk Ll Mm Nn Oo Pp Qq Rr Ss Tt Uu Vv Ww Xx Yy Zz

11

Kk

Katydid

Katydids rub their front wings together to sing. They have ears on their legs to hear the sounds of other katydids.

Ladybugs eat bugs that eat plants, so gardeners like them. When something tries to eat the ladybug, though, the ladybug pulls its head inside its red and black shell and squirts out a bitter orange juice.

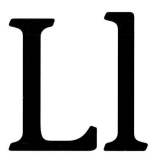

Ladybug

Mm

Moving Leaf

The moving leaf is a bug that eats leaves. The moving leaf looks so much like a leaf itself that other leaf-eating bugs sometimes take a bite out of it.

A nut weevil has a long, thin tube with mouth parts on the end, which it uses to make a hole in a nut. Once the nut weevil's tube is inside the nut, it lays its egg there. When the baby nut weevil hatches, it eats its way out of the nut.

Nn

Nut Weevil

Oo

Ocean Strider

Ocean striders skim along the surface of the ocean water. They have tiny hairs on the bottoms of their feet, which work like snowshoes to keep them on top of the water.

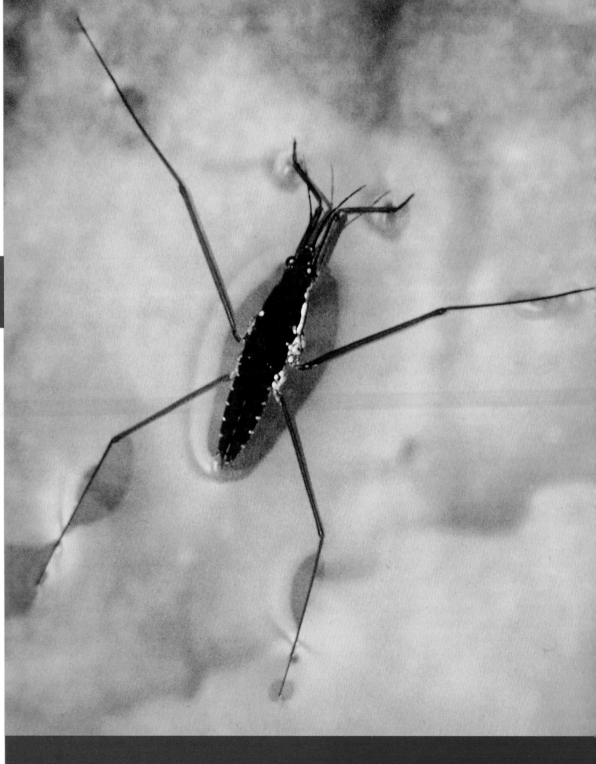

The praying mantis is a good fighter. It uses its front legs to grab and hold. The praying mantis will stand up to other bugs, mammals, and even people. It can even turn its head so that it faces completely backwards!

Pp

Praying Mantis

Aa Bb Cc Dd Ee Ff Gg Hh Ii Jj Kk Ll Mm Nn Oo **Pp** Qq Rr Ss Tt Uu Vv Ww Xx Yy Zz

Qq

The Queen Butterfly lays its eggs on milkweed plants. After the eggs hatch, the caterpillars eat the poisonous milkweed. The poison makes the caterpillar, and then the butterfly, taste bad.

Queen Butterfly

Aa Bb Cc Dd Ee Ff Gg Hh Ii Jj Kk Ll Mm Nn Oo Pp **Qq** Rr Ss Tt Uu Vv Ww Xx Yy Zz

Rr

Red Widow Spider

Red widow spiders belong to the same family as the black widow spider. They are both extremely poisonous, so please don't try to pet them.

Ss

The silkworm is the larva, or baby, of the silk moth. The silkworm spins a strong silk cocoon around its body when it is time to change into a moth. One silkworm caterpillar can make a silk thread 5,000 feet long!

Silkworm

Tt

Termite

Termites live in and eat old or rotting wood. A colony, or group, of termites includes a queen. The queen's responsibility is to lay eggs. She can lay an egg every three seconds and lives for 15 years. That's a lot of eggs!

Aa Bb Cc Dd Ee Ff Gg Hh Ii Jj Kk Ll Mm Nn Oo Pp Qq Rr Ss **Tt** Uu Vv Ww Xx Yy Zz

21

Uu

The umber moth caterpillar is camouflaged to look like a stick. When danger is near, it climbs between a branch and the stem of a plant to hide. It looks more like a stick than a tasty snack.

Umber Moth Caterpillar

Vv

Viceroy Butterfly

The viceroy butterfly is orange and black. In nature, these colors mean that something will taste bitter. The viceroy butterfly, however, does not really taste bitter. It just tricks the birds and bugs to make them think it does.

Ww

Walking Stick

The walking stick looks just like a small stick. Walking sticks are brown or green and can grow to be two to three inches long (five to eight centimeters). Walking sticks live and hide from enemies in leaves and branches.

Xylocopa is the scientific name for the carpenter bee. Scientists put bugs into groups. The word part *xylo* means *wood*. Xylocopa means *a bee that lives in wood.*

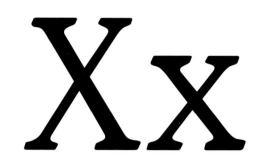

Xylocopa

Yy

Yucca Moth

The yucca moth and the yucca plant need each other. The yucca moth spreads the yucca flower's pollen. The yucca flower is a nest for the yucca moth to lay its eggs. This is teamwork!

The zebra tarantula finds a hole in the ground and covers it with a trap door, such as a leaf. When a bug, or dinner, steps on the trap door, it falls through, and the zebra tarantula attacks.

Zz

Zebra Tarantula

Note To Teachers and Parents

Bugs A to Z introduces children to the world of bugs while building mastery of the alphabet. The combination of alphabetic knowledge and real-world facts makes learning the ABCs fun. The real-life photographs and fascinating facts encourage lively discussions that develop oral language skills, extend science concepts, as well as develop phonological awareness and alphabetic skills. In addition, the lists of web sites, the bibliography, and a hands-on project bring this book's information to learners of all styles.

Hands-On Project

My Bugs A to Z

Invite children to create their own ABC books or posters. Set up a 26-column chart headed by the letters of the alphabet. Place the names of the bugs in *Bugs A to Z* as the first bug on each of the lists. Have children list the names of other bugs and put them in the correct column. Once the chart is complete, have children select their favorite bugs to create their own ABC books or posters. Use photographs from magazines, web sites, or children's drawings to illustrate the books or posters.

Develop Phonological Awareness

Use the chart developed in *My Bugs A to Z* to play a game of *What Doesn't Belong*. To play the game, say the names of three bugs. Two of the bugs need to begin with the same letter sound. The third word needs to clearly begin with a different letter sound. For example:

monarch, mosquito, grasshopper

bedbug, bumble bee, ant

termite, weevil, tarantula

Have a volunteer explain which bug doesn't belong and name the initial sound for the other two. As children get good at this game, challenge them to play it in a learning center with a partner or small group.

Internet Sites

Butterfly Web Site: http://www.butterflywebsite.com

Insects: http://www.nosweat.com

The Yuckiest Bug Site: http://www.yucky.com

Books

Imes, Rick. *Incredible BUGS. The Ultimate Guide to the World of Insects.* New York, NY: Barnes & Noble Books, 1997.

McCormick, Rosemary. *Insects and Spiders.* New York, NY: Dorling Kindersley, Inc., 1993.

Mound, Laurence. *Eyewitness Books Insect.* New York, NY: Dorling Kindersley, Inc., 1990.

Phillips, Sarah. *What's Inside? Insects.* New York, NY: Dorling Kindersley, Inc., 1992.

Purcell, Geraldine. *Weird and Wonderful Insects.* New York, NY: Thomson Learning, 1991.

Whayne, Susanne Santoro. *The World of Insects.* New York, NY: Simon & Schuster Books for Young Readers, 1990.

Glossary

Ants

- Ants can be black, brown, red, or yellow
- Most ants nest in a system of tunnels in the soil, often under a hill
- Ant colonies have anywhere from a dozen to half a million ants

Aphids

- Aphids are under ¼ inch (6mm) long
- Most aphids live on the stems or leaves of plants
- Aphids live in colonies that vary in size from dozens to thousands

Bedbugs

- Bedbugs belong to the *Cimicidae* family that includes about 30 species
- Bedbugs are flat-bodied, oval, reddish brown, and about ¼ inch (6mm) long
- Bedbugs live in bedding, bird nests, and other warm, dry places

Centipede

- Centipedes live in the ground, in litter, and under logs or rocks
- Centipedes are from 1 inch (2.5cm) to as long as 1 foot (30cm)
- Centipedes eat mainly bugs, but the larger ones will attack small mammals

Dragonfly

- Dragonflies live throughout the world except in the polar regions
- Most dragonflies live where it is very warm
- Dragonflies vary in size from 1–5 inches (2–13cm) long

Earwig

- Earwigs get their name from an old superstition that they would climb into peoples' ears while they slept
- Earwigs have a pair of horny pincers on their abdomens
- There are 900 kinds of earwigs

Firefly

- Fireflies are nocturnal (they come out at night) beetles
- Firefly larvae and wingless females are called glowworms
- Some types of fireflies glow while in the egg

Grasshopper

- There are 9,000 different kinds of grasshoppers
- Grasshoppers range from ½–4 inches (1–10cm) long
- The largest grasshoppers can jump more than 6 feet (1.5m)

Honeybee

- Honeybees have large back feet with baskets made of stiff hairs for gathering pollen
- Honeybees make their hives in crevices or hollow trees
- Many plants need bees to spread their pollen, or they will not survive

Inchworm

- Inchworms are the larvae of the *Geometridae* family of moths
- There are more than 1,200 types of inchworms
- Inchworms are about 1 inch (2.5cm) long

Jewel Beetle

- Jewel beetles live on trees, bushes, and plants
- It is also called the metallic or round-headed wood-boring beetle
- The family is found worldwide, with species on all continents including many Pacific islands

Katydid

- Katydids belong to the long-horned grasshopper family
- Katydids are green or sometimes pink, and range in size from 1–5 inches (3–13cm) long
- Katydids are nocturnal (they sing in the evening)

Ladybug

- Ladybugs are a type of beetle (there are over 4,000 kinds of beetles)
- Ladybugs are ¼ inch (6mm) long
- Ladybugs can be red or yellow with black spots, or black with red or yellow spots

Moving Leaf

- The moving leaf is green and has a flat, leaf-shaped body
- The moving leaf is about 4 inches (10cm) long
- The moving leaf lives in tropical places

Nut Weevil

- Nut weevils are also called acorn weevils
- Nut weevils are about ½ inch (8mm) long
- Adult nut weevils also like to eat fruit

Ocean Strider

- The ocean strider is the only species of insect that lives in the ocean
- Ocean striders eat zooplankton, a tiny plant
- Ocean striders lay their eggs on feathers and other things that float in the water

Praying Mantis

- While waiting for prey, a praying mantis holds its front legs in a way that makes it look as though it were praying
- The adult praying mantis can grow as large as 5 inches (13cm) long
- The praying mantis is either green or brown

Queen Butterfly

- Queen Butterflies lay single eggs on milkweed plants
- The poisons from the milkweed make the caterpillar and butterfly taste bad to birds and other predators

- After eating a Queen Butterfly or caterpillar, a predator will remember the bright colors and the bad taste and leave it alone

Red Widow Spider

- The red widow spider is about 2 inches (5cm) long with its legs extended
- The red widow spider has a reddish orange head/thorax and legs and a black abdomen
- Like most spiders, red widow spiders are shy and will not bite unless aggravated

Silkworm

- Mature silkworms, 38 days old, are about 3 inches (7.5cm) long
- Silkworms live in Asia and Africa
- Silkworms are hatched from eggs so small that 35,000 of them weigh 1 ounce (28g)

Termite

- There are 2,000 species of termites
- Some kinds of termites build huge mounds to house their colonies
- The mounds, up to 40 feet (12m) tall, are found in Africa and Australia

Umber Moth Caterpillar

- The umber moth caterpillar eats birch and oak trees
- The umber moth caterpillar has a wingspan of ½–4 inches (1.5–10cm)
- The umber moth caterpillar lives from Maine to Florida, and west to Wisconsin and east Texas

Viceroy Butterfly

- Viceroy butterflies live mainly in the tops of cottonwood trees
- Viceroy butterflies are found throughout the United States
- The viceroy butterfly looks a lot like the monarch butterfly, which protects it from predators

Walking Stick

- Adult walking sticks can be shorter than 1 inch to more than 1 foot (2–33cm) long
- Walking sticks can regrow legs when they lose them
- Walking sticks can be found in Asia and the warmer parts of Europe and North America

Xylocopa

- Carpenter bees are about 1 inch (2.5cm) long
- Carpenter bees will build nests in houses, fences, and most other wooden things
- Carpenter bees' nests have been known to be in use for as long as 14 years

Yucca Moth

- The wingspan of the yucca moth is generally ¾ inch (2cm)
- The color of the yucca moth is similar to the color of the yucca plant to protect it from predators
- The yucca moth lives in the Northern Hemisphere in places where the yucca plant grows

Zebra Tarantula

- The adult zebra tarantula is about 4 inches (10cm) long
- Zebra tarantulas live in the southern United States and Central America
- Zebra tarantulas live in burrows under plants and trees

Index

A+ Books are published by Capstone Press
P.O. Box 669, Mankato, Minnesota 56002
http://www.capstone-press.com

EDITORIAL CREDITS:

Susan Evento, Managing Editor/Product Development; Don L. Curry, Senior Editor; Jannike Hess, Designer; Kimberly Danger and Heidi Schoof, Photo Researchers; Content Consultant: Mark O'Brien

LIBRARY OF CONGRESS CATALOGING-IN-PUBLICATION DATA

DeGezelle, Terri, 1955-
    Bugs A to Z/by Terri DeGezelle
      p.   cm.
    Includes bibliographical references.
    Summary: Introduces the world of bugs through photographs and facts which describe one for each letter of the alphabet.
    ISBN 0-7368-7036-9 (hard) — ISBN 0-7368-7050-4 (paper)
    1. Insects–Juvenile literature. 2. Arthropoda–Juvenile literature. 3. English language–Alphabet–Juvenile literature. [1. Insects. 2. Arthropods. 3. Alphabet.] I. Title.
    QL467.2 .D44 2000
    595.7–dc21
                            99-052407

PHOTO CREDITS:

Cover: James P. Rowan; *Title Page:* J. Gerholdt; *Page 2:* Robert & Linda Mitchell; *Page 3:* Bill Beatty; *Page 4:* Rob & Ann Simpson; *Page 5:* Lynn M. Stone; *Page 6:* Bill Johnson; *Page 7:* Dwight Kuhn; *Page 8:* James P. Rowan; *Page 9:* Dwight Kuhn; *Page 10:* James P. Rowan; *Page 11:* Michael Turco; *Page 12:* Dwight Kuhn; *Page 13:* Robert & Linda Mitchell; *Page 14:* Robert & Linda Mitchell; *Page 15:* Kjell B. Sandved/Visuals Unlimited; *Page 16:* P. Starborn/Visuals Unlimited; *Page 17:* Janet Haas; *Page 18:* Paul Rezendes; *Page 19:* Joe Warfel; *Page 20:* Dwight Kuhn; *Page 21:* Dwight Kuhn; *Page 22:* K. Silvonen; *Page 23:* Robert McCaw; *Page 24:* James P. Rowan; *Page 25:* Doug Wechsler; *Page 26:* Robert & Linda Mitchell; *Page 27:* Robert & Linda Mitchell